My World War Two Adventures In Denmark

Carsten R Jorgensen

ISBN:
ISBN-13: 978-0-9949338-2-9
ISBN-10: 0-9949338-2-7

DEDICATION

This book is dedicated to my Father, Ejvind (Ivan) Reinholdt Jorgensen and the Danish Police in World War Two.

CONTENTS

ACKNOWLEDGMENTS

My daughter Dana Woodard helped me with the pictures. I really appreciate Dana's work on the cover of this book.

1. AIR RAID

The air raid sounded loud and long, rising in pitch, falling again and rising in pitch and falling again over and over. "OOOOooaaaAAAAOOOooaaaAAAOOOooaaa"

Everybody in our apartment building went to the basement. I was placed on top of a cabinet in a type of basket. There I stared up at the water pipes running along the ceiling. Many water pipes! They were so close that I could touch them which I did not do. I felt uncomfortable there and I hated it.

Some days later it happened again. The air raid sounded. We went to the basement. I was placed on top of the cabinet in a bassinet where I stared at the water pipes.

Many times this event happened. When I was a grown man I remembered this event. I told my mother that I had these dreams about when I was small and I described them to her. She said, "Those were not dreams. When you were an infant and the air raid sounded we went to the basement. We placed you in a bassinet and placed you on top of a cabinet."

At that time we lived in an apartment at Thyregodsvej 18 in the district of Valby in the city of Copenhagen. The apartment had five stories and the building was attached to the next apartment building. That apartment building was attached to the next apartment building. This kept on so that the apartment buildings covered a city block.

Outside our apartment building if you looked to the right up the street you could see the Valby bus station. Just beyond that was the Valby train station. If you looked down the street the other way, you could see more apartment buildings. If you walked down the street in that direction and turned the corner to the left there were shops. The first was a bakery shop.

When entering our apartment building, there were stairs. On the right the stairs went to the basement where we went during air raids. On the left were five steps going up. At the top of the stairs were the doors to two apartments. The first door was the entrance to our home. Stairs going further up also led to two more apartment entrances. There were five floors of two apartment entrances. All the apartment buildings were laid out in this fashion.

Across the street from us were apartment buildings laid out in the same pattern as the one in which we lived. The one across the street had the large entrance to the yard facing us. In Valby there were many blocks of apartment buildings all constructed in this pattern.

Just outside the entrance to our apartment building on the right was a wide entrance which led into a yard that was surrounded by the apartment buildings. Inside the yard were swings, teeter totters and at one end there was an area people could use to beat the dust and dirt from their rugs. This was an iron pole supported by a pole on each end. Children played in the yard, most of the time unattended by adults.

In the yard where children played were concrete stairs going down to the basement. This consisted of two sets of stairs along the wall going down to a concrete floor. This formed a sort of pit. The door to the basement was in the wall at the middle of the pit. There was an iron railing consisting of two bars running across the top of the pit to keep people from falling down and the stairs had an iron banister.

These were my first memories.

2. ROMANCE DURING THE OCCUPATION

My parents met at the Baptist High School in Tollose Sjaelland. Along with his studies, my Father, Ivan Reinholdt Jorgensen, did some gardening for the principal.

Baptist High School in Tollose

My father's parents lived in the city of Odense on the island of Fyn. He was the second of seven boys. My mother's parents lived on the island of Mors in the Lim Fjord in Jutland (Jylland). My mother, Vera Elfrida Dam, was the youngest of four girls. She also had two younger brothers.

While attending the baptist high school, my mother not only met Ivan but she met another young man, Sigurd, as well. These two men both wanted a relationship with Vera. However, Ivan wanted to become a missionary in Africa and because Vera did not want to go to Africa, she developed a relationship with Sigurd instead.

After leaving high school, Vera worked at a tourist resort called Liseleje which was located on the Kattegat coast on north Sjaelland. The owners were the Larsens, (Mrs.) Fru Larsen and Hovmester Larsen. Hovmester is a title of someone in charge of fancy menus and foods. The King's butler has the title Hovmester. (Fru = Mrs. Froken = Miss)

Liseleje Tourist Resort

In 1939 Denmark signed a non-aggression pact with Germany. When this went on the news, my mother's brother, Herman said, "Lets see if we can hold ourselves back and not attack Germany."

On April 9, 1940, just after four o'clock in the morning the sound of many airplanes could be heard from the sky. The sky in Denmark became dark with German war planes flying into the country. At the same time the German army entered into Jutland.

The German army marched into Jutland

German ships disembarked soldiers at Assens, Middlefart and Nyborg in Fyn. There were also troops disembarking at Korsor in south Sjaelland. German war planes flew to the Danish air force in Aalborg. One Danish war plane managed to take off but it was shot down. The rest of the planes were destroyed on the ground. Many of the German planes went on to Norway which also became occupied by the Germans.

At Langelinie in Copenhagen a German assault battalion had disembarked. At Amalienborg the Danish Royal Guard were firing at German troops in the palace square. At six o'clock King Christian X ordered his Royal Guards to cease firing. The King and his ministers had agreed to the German demands. The streets in Copenhagen were full of German soldiers.

At mid morning King Christian went on the radio and advised his people to go about their normal business and not to worry. Then the Germans had a Danish radio announcer tell the Danes the conditions of the occupation. First he said, "We the German soldiers are here to protect you from Britain."

One of the conditions was that at night there must be no light whatsoever in Denmark. There must be no light at all to guide British bombers. British bomber planes would fly over Denmark at night and bomb German headquarters and factories making arms, bombs and ammunition for the Germans. To achieve this condition a blanket must cover every window in Denmark at night.

The occupation of Denmark was a difficult time for the police. When problems arose between citizens and German soldiers did the police have jurisdiction? How would these problems be resolved? Just before the war had started Ivan Jorgensen had become a police officer in Copenhagen. He now had to face these difficulties.

Police Officer Ivan Jorgensen

Vera's boyfriend, Sigurd, wanted to be a soldier. It was his life's ambition. But the Danish army no longer existed, so to satisfy his ambition, Sigurd wanted to travel into Germany to join the German army. The Danish Nazi party had created a soldier group called Free Corps Denmark. This Group enlisted Danish volunteers who were Nazi sympathizers. In this way Sigurd became a soldier by volunteering to join Free Corps Denmark and was sent to Germany for basic training. This did not sit well with my mother.

My mother wanted nothing to do with Sigurd any more. He was a Nazi sympathizer and a traitor. Instead, she attended a highschool reunion where she met up with Ivan and they rekindled their relationship. On Saturday, August 2, 1941 Vera Dam and Ivan Jorgensen were married. They moved into an apartment at Thyregodsvej 18 in the district of Valby in Copenhagen.

Ivan and Vera Jorgensen

The resistance to the German occupation started slowly. Underground newspapaers started up. Teenagers wrote anti German graffiti and slogans on fences and walls. Later young adults and teenagers demonstrated against the Germans.

In Aalborg at the end of 1941, a 17 year old school boy, Knud Pedersen formed a club called the Churchill Club. The club had eight members. All of them were teenage school boys. It carried out acts of sabotage against the Germans.

The Churchill Club was the first organized resistance group.

The Germans took over the Valby bus station which was at the end of our street. A group of teenagers gathered at the end of the street to demonstrate against the Germans taking over the bus station. As my mother was watching from the apartment window, a German army truck drove by on the street. It stopped and let off one lone soldier with a machine gun. Then the truck proceeded out of the street. The soldier started to sneak up on the demonstrators. My mother ran out of the apartment and down the five steps of the stairs. Then she opened the glass door to the street and stepped out into the street. When my mother yelled a warning to the demonstrators, the soldier turned and fired his machine gun at her. My mother missed getting hit by jumping inside. The glass of the door shattered with the impact of the bullets.

3. THYREGODSVEJ 18

In 1942 the German Reich relied upon the Danish agriculture to supply the 3.6 million Germans with meat, milk, and butter. In the winter the Germans emptied the Danish store houses. Food for the Danes became very limited and food was rationed. To buy food you needed to have ration coupons. Butter was completely unavailable. People had to use margarine.

On April 17, 1942 I was born at home. A midwife had helped in the delivery. My Mother later told me that when my Father first saw me, he turned to my Mother and said, "Don't you think he looks like me?"

Me and my Mother

I could walk when I was nine months old. This changed life for me. One day I was at the railroad station walking with my mother. A man stopped, watched me walk and asked my mother, "How old is your boy?"

"Nine months", replied my Mother.

"That is a lie.", replied the man.

Me and my Mother

On the fifth floor lived a girl my age. Her name was Alice. Alice's father was a bus driver. Alice was my first friend and I visited her very often. One day while visiting Alice, she pulled out a box and emptied it on the floor. The box had been full of sea shells. We played for a long time with the shells until I had to go home.

There were three notable events in 1942. In May all eight members of the Churchill Club were arrested by the police. They were charged $1,860 million for destroying Nazi property. They were also given prison sentences ranging from two to three years.

The Churchill Club members were put in prison.

In prison they escaped at night and continued their sabotage activity. During the day the Churchill Club boys did their studies in jail. There were no distractions so they were able to concentrate on their school studies. Later they said that because of the jail time their school marks improved.

On May 8, Free Corps Danmark was ordered to the Eastern Front. There Sigurd was killed by the Russian army along with 4,000 members of Free Corps Denmark.

The third notable event was the formation of the Holger Danske group in Copenhagen. This group was formed by veteran volunteers from the Winter War in Finland. The name of the group was chosen because Holger Danske is a legendary Danish Hero. He sleeps in the basement of Kronborg Castle.

Holger Danske asleep in Kronborg Castle

The author Hans Christian Andersen wrote about him and said that when Denmark is in trouble Holger Danske will wake up and fight the enemies of Denmark. The Holger Danske Group founders decided that it was time for Holger Danske to wake up, therefore they took his name.

Two members of Holger Danske were Jorgen Haagen Schmith and Bent Faurschou-Hviid.

Jorgen Haagen Schmith..... code name: Flammen (The Flame)

Jorgen's code name was Flammen (The Flame) because of his red hair.

Bent's code name was Citronen (the Citron) because that was the brand of car he drove.

Bent Faurschou-Hviid.......code name: Citronen (the Citron)

Holger Danske was very active in 1943 and 1944. It carried out about 100 sabotage operations and executed about 200 informers (stikker).

(In 2008 a movie was made about Jorgen and Bent. It was called "Flammen og Citronen". The part of Flammen was played by Thure Lindhart. Citronen was played by Mads Kikkelsen.)

4. A STATE OF EMERGENCY

In March 1943 Denmark held an election and the democratic parties won the election. The Germans made the demand of the government that there be a death penalty for saboteurs but the government refused. So there was no death penalty in Denmark.

The British Captain Ole Giesler of the Special Operations Executive (SOE) met with the owner of the Hvidsten Inn, Marius Fils, on March 12, 1943. The Hvidsten Inn lay between Randers and Mariager in Jutland. The SOE arranged to have containers of explosives and weapons air dropped in Jutland. Marius Fils became the leader of a resistance group called the Hvidsten Group.

The Hvidsten Group received many drops of explosives and weapons. The times and places of the drops were announced in code at the end of BBC news broadcasts starting with "Greetings to Elias- Listen again".

The Hvidsten Group picked up the weapons and explosive packages and delivered them to many resistance groups including Holger Danske. The explosives were used to blow up railways, locomotives, bridges, and factories servicing the Nazis.

In mid 1943 the battle of Stalingrad took place. This caused the Danish communists to become more active. They formed their own resistance groups. The Danish resistance movement became more assertive in its underground press and sabotage activity increased. In the summer several nation wide strikes took place and there were armed confrontations between Danes and German troops.

On August 28 the co-operation between Germany and the Danish government ended. The German in charge of Denmark, SS General Werner Best declared Denmark to be in a state of emergency.

The measures proclaimed for the "state of emergency" were as follows:

"Public meetings of more than five persons are prohibited.

Any form of strike or any form of support of strikers are prohibited.

Any form of gathering or meeting in a closed room or in the open air is prohibited. There will be a curfew between the hours of 8:30 p.m. And 5:30 a.m. All restaurants will close at 7:30 p.m.

All weapons and explosives will be surrendered before September 1, 1943. Any encroachment on the rights of Danish citizens as a result of their own or their relatives' co-operation with the German authorities, or relationships with Germans, is prohibited.

There will be a censorship of the Press under German control.

Summary courts will be set up to deal with cases where the above-mentioned decrees are violated to the prejudice of security and order.

Violation of the above-mentioned decrees shall be severely punished under the laws which empower the government to maintain order and security. Any sabotage and all assistance in sabotage, any defiance of the German Wehrmacht and its members, as well as continued retention of weapons and explosives after the first of September, will be subject to the death penalty immediately.

The German government expects the Danish government to accept the above-mentioned demands before 1600 hours today."

The Danish government with the approval of the King sent a polite reply to Werner Best stating that it regretted that it can not find it right to help in carrying through these provisions. The next day, August 29, about one hundred prominent Danes were taken hostage. In response the Danish government resigned. Now the German authorities had direct administration of Denmark..

German troops attacked the Danish army. The Danish navy scuttled its own ships. German soldiers stood guard at all the important buildings including the King's palace. Mail, telephone and telegraph service was stopped.

In September the Danish Freedom Council was formed. This was an attempt to unify all the different resistance groups. The main leaders moved to Sweden. Stockholm became a base for the Danish resistance.

5. THE JEWS

On September 28, 1943 a German Diplomat, Georg Ferdinand Duckwitz leaked word to former members of the Danish government that there were plans to round up and deport all the Danish Jews. The date set for the roundup was during the night of October 1. Word of this spread all over Denmark.

Danes independently found Jews and hid them. In Copenhagen there were people who walked out into the streets to find Jews. They would give Jews the keys to their apartments and told them to go and hide there. Jews were being hid in homes, churches, school houses and hospitals. The Jews who were hidden in hospitals were brought there by ambulance.

My mother's parents who lived on the island of Mors in the Lim Fjord in Jutland took in a young Jewish woman named Ruth.

On the night of October 1, the Germans could find no Jews.

My Mother is on the left. Ruth is on the right.

My Mothers parents Nielssigne (Signe) and Niels Dam.
My Mormor (Mother's Mother) and Morfar (Mother's Father)
Niels Dam was a mail man.

NIELS BOHR

Niels Bohr was a Danish physicist. His theory of the atom was revolutionary. In the United States of America, the Jewish German scientist, Albert Einstein, told the Americans that in order to build the atomic bomb they would need the Danish phycisist Niels Bohr and that they should try to get him before Germany did.

Niels Bohr

The Nazis considered Bohr to be Jewish. The Danish resistance brought Niels Bohr across the Ore Sound to Sweden where an airplane was waiting to take him to the United States. However, Niels refused to board the plane because he wanted an audience with King Gustav V before he left. He worked hard to get an audience but he was unable to succeed.

Niels and King Gustav V had a mutual friend, the Swedish movie star, Greta Garbo. Niels got together with Greta and told her of his difficulties. Greta went directly to Gustav V and persuaded the King to grant an audience with Niels Bohr.

Greta Garbo

King Gustav V of Sweden

Niels persuaded the Swedish King to announce that Sweden was ready to accept Danish Jews. The Swedish consulate in Denmark began to make Swedish passports for the Danish Jews.

Niels Bohr then flew to the United States to work on the Manhattan project in Los Almos, New Mexico.

The resistance people as well as private citizens found fishermen willing to ferry Jews from Denmark to Sweden. There was a German vessel in the Copenhagen harbour waiting to take on Jews to be transported to Germany. The Harbor Master ordered the ship into dry dock for repairs. German patrol boats were also ordered into dry dock. Then the Harbor Master had his vessel filled with Jews and had his son take the ship to Sweden.

The Danish police and the Danish coast guard co-operated with the rescue efforts. The Danish coast guard would radio the locations of German patrol boats to the Danish police who would tell the fishing boat captains where the patrol boats were located.

My father's patrol area included Nyhavn. In Nyhavn there is a canal running from the Ore Sound right into Copenhagen where there is a port for ocean going vessels. There were many fishing boats docking at this harbor. Ivan Jorgensen helped Jews reach these fishing boats.

One day in Nyhavn, Ivan stepped into a bar to check it out. The bar was full of German soldiers drinking Tuborg beer. A soldier came running into the bar and yelled, "Quick! There is a fishing boat outside being loaded with Jews! Let's go out and catch them!"

The commander of the soldiers yelled, "No! Everybody stay where you are! It is not our job to round up Jews. We are soldiers of the Reich! The rounding up of the Jews is the job of the Gestapo. Everybody sit down and have another drink. That is an order!"
Then he bought a round for his men.

It was not always easy for the Jews to sail to Sweden. Fishermen had to keep an eye out for floating mines and German patrol boats. When approached by a patrol boat, some fishing boats would throw their nets into the water to appear as though they were fishing. The patrol boat would then pass by them. The fishing boat would have to fish for a couple of hours making the trip to Sweden longer. Meanwhile the hold of the boat, stinking with the smell of fish, would be crammed full of Jews.

On October 6, the Gestapo entered a Lutheran church in Gilleleje. They captured 80 Jews hiding in the loft of the church. They had been given up by an informer (stikker). This stikker was a young woman in love with a German soldier.

By the end of October 7,220 of Denmark's 7,800 Jews had evacuated to Sweden. In addition 686 non-Jewish spouses had gone with them. 580 Jews failed to escape to Sweden. 464 were captured and put into concentration camps. Of the rest, some remained hidden until the end of the war. Some died in accidents and a few committed suicide.

6. THE PETER GROUP

In late 1943, groups of Nazi sympathizers became more active and formed groups called Schalburg Corps. These groups did retaliation killings and counter-sabotage. The most active was the Peter Group. Counter-sabotage was called schalburgtage by the Danes. Schalburgtage was directed against both the Danish resistance movement and the Danish society in general. When a German soldier or a stikker was killed, Schalburg men would carry out the killing of a prominent Dane in society.

On December 18 the British army paratrooper, Jacob Jansen, employed by the SOE was captured. He was interrogated under torture on March 11, 1944. and he gave up the Hvidsten Group. The Gestapo surrounded Hvidsten Inn and captured most of the group. On June 26, 1944 eight of the Hvidsten group were sentenced to death. They were executed by firing squad on June 29, three weeks after D day.

KAI MONK

Kai Munk was a Danish Lutheran Minister. He was also a famous playwright and produced many plays for the Danish theater. The Danes loved him. In church Kai preached sermons against the Nazis. In 1938 in the Danish newspaper, Jyllands-Posten, Kai Monk had written an open letter to Benito Mussolini criticizing the persecution against Jews.

Kai Munk preached against Danes who were collaborating with the Germans. His friends urged him to go underground but Kai did not listen. He continued to preach against the Danes who were collaborating with the Germans. Kai Munk was arrested by the Gestapo on January 4, 1944.

Kai Munk

The next morning Kai Munk's body was found in a roadside ditch near Silkeborg. Four thousand Danes attended Kai Munk's funeral. His body was returned to his Parish church. A simple stone cross was erected on a small hill overlooking the site where his body had been dumped.

In January half of the issue of the resistance paper, "De Frie Danske" was devoted to Kai Munk. His portrait filled the front page. The next page was filled with his obituary. The New Years Sermon he had given was on the next page. The page after gave a report of his murder and there were pictures of his funeral..

His widow, Lise, was allowed by the Danish government to live in the parish house until she died in 1998.

On April 17 I turned two years old. My parents thought I was old enough to play in the yard unattended by an adult. My father laid down rules for me to follow. I was never to go on the road but to keep on the sidewalk when not in the yard. I was forbidden to be on the inside of the railing at the stairs to the basements. There were grilled lids to the storm sewers and I was to never open one. These grilled lids permitted water to run into the storm sewers during heavy rain.

There had been cases when a grilled lid was open that a child had fallen into the open shaft. On the last occasion which was announced on the radio, the little two year old boy had died. The shafts leading down to the sewage systems were very narrow and would make it impossible for an adult to fall into. It was also impossible for a two year old boy to fall into one. I think he would have had to crawl into it. If he had, it would have been imposible for him to crawl out again because of the narrowness of the shaft. Some of these shafts were not quite as deep. I once saw a boy a little older than me open a grill and get into the shaft. He did not go any deeper than up to his waist when standing.

I met some boys my own age who became my friends. They were Soren, Jorgen, Sten, Ole, and Mogens.

In good weather I was outside playing with my friends. One day, to my horror, I came across Soren standing on the inside of a basement railing. I told him that this was not allowed. He just looked at me. Then I told him that my father had told me it was not allowed and that my father was a police man and therefore it was definitely not allowed. Soren ignored me. Therefore I pushed him off the railing. Soren was taken to the hospital. He had a concussion.

One day I came out to play and there was Soren with one of the grilled lids open. I went over and slammed the lid shut. Soren's thumb got caught between the lid and the shaft. Soren was again taken to the hospital. He had his thumb reconstructed.

One day me and my gang went into an apartment building where none of us lived. We ran up and down the stairs playing games. A man came out of one of the apartments and yelled at us. We became terrified and ran down the stairs and out the door. Soren was a little bit slower than the rest of us. When he reached the door it was almost closed. Soren ran right through the glass in the door. Once again Soren was taken to the hospital. He had multiple glass cuts.

I am on the far left in the second row. Next to me is Soren. In the second row third from the right is Sten. To the left of Sten is Alice. In the back row, the third person from the left is Manse, Sten's older brother. On the extreme right is seen the first step leading down into a basement. Behind the children is the two bar iron railing. Some of the boys are sitting on this railing.

In the evenings after supper my father sometimes played the violin. Years later I read the Sherlock Holmes stories. I read that Sherlock Holmes played the violin. After that, Sherlock Holmes looked like my father in my imagination.

We had a record player. This record player was not run on electricity; you had to wind it up. My mother played Danish songs on it. One of my favourites was "Hyp Lille Lotte" ("Giddy Up Little Lotte"). It was about a little horse who pulled a taxi buggy in Copenhagen. My mother's favourite song was "Skamlinsbanken".

At Christmas, 1944, our neighbours on the third floor, Hr. and Fru Kristiansen invited me up for a visit. It was fascinating. Hr Kristiansen had made a model of a village. The ground was all snow (cotton batten). He had a little village with houses in which the lights could be turned on with a switch. There was a pond made from a mirror with the edges covered with cotton batten so that the non-mirror parts were not seen. There were little elves (jule nisser) made from red wool and wearing little red hats. Some elves were on skis with the skis and ski poles made from match sticks. There were elves skating on the pond on skates made of broken match sticks.

One of my Christmas presents was a sleigh. It was not a big sleigh, but just big enough for one person my size to sit on it. One day after the holiday season, my mother and I walked to a little park with the sleigh. Denmark is very flat, but in that park was a little hill. We walked to the top of the hill where I got on the sleigh and went sliding down the hill. I thought this was lots of fun. My mother helped me get the sleigh back on top of the hill and I slid down again. We did this several times. When we were walking home, my mother told me that the hill was a Viking burial mound.

My mother used her alarm clock to teach me how to tell time. She adjusted the hands on the clock and told me what time it was. After a while she adjusted the hands on the clock and I told her what time it was.

When I went out to play in the yard, I skipped the last step on the stairs. I jumped over it. Later I jumped over two stair steps. Eventually when I left the apartment I would jump over all five stair steps (when I was not accompanied by an adult).

One day my mother called me to the living room window. There just below the window was a strange boy who was not from our yard. He was much older and taller than me. He was holding a big stick in his left hand and he was throwing stones at our window with his right hand. My Mother was upset at him throwing stones and she said, "If he throws a stone hard enough it will break the window."

Then she said "Go out and chase him away." I said "But he is bigger than me and he has a big stick." My mother replied, "I can not chase him away because I am an adult. All those children would report me and I would be in trouble."

I looked out the window and sure enough there were many children from our yard gathered and they were standing there watching him. I said, "That stick is big and he is bigger than me."

My mother said, "That does not matter. You go out and hit him with your fists as hard as you can. Keep hitting him till he runs away."

I went out of the apartment. This time I did not jump the five steps but walked down slowly while I imagined this big boy beating me with the stick. When I got outside I stood and looked at the big boy. I took a deep breath. I glanced up and saw my mother looking out the window. Then I ran at the big boy and hit him with my fists as hard as I could. I was surprised that this big boy never fought back. He did not even try to hit me.

I managed to hit the boy three times. Then he ran. No, he sprinted as fast as his legs could carry him and kept running until he was out of sight. The children who were watching cheered for me.

7. THE KING

On the day of the German invasion King Christian had gone on the radio and told the Danish people to not aggravate the Germans but to go on about their lives as normal. All the Danes loved their King and he loved all the Danes.

The King went about his normal business. Every day he rode his horse through the streets of Copenhagen. People would line the streets to watch him ride by. When people waved or saluted at him, he saluted back. When he would come to a red light, he would stop until the light turned green.

One day in 1944, my mother decided that we should go downtown and see the King. My father was at work. My mother and I walked down our street to the bus station so we could get on a bus to go downtown.

There was a line up of people wanting to get on the bus. We took our place at the end of the line. A man came walking from the street. He did not stop at the end of the line but walked along the line until he reached a man way ahead of us. He looked closely at the man. Then he shot him with a pistol and walked away. A member of Holger Danske had just executed an informer.

When we arrived downtown we found a street which was part of the King's route. The street was full of people including German soldiers.

We waited and saw the King come riding.

King Christian X

The Danish people cheered when they saw the King. They waved Danish flags and some people saluted him. The King saluted the Danes who waved or saluted. When Germans saluted him, King

Christian ignored them. I was standing beside a boy older than me. He was probably nine or ten. A German soldier standing on the other side of the boy said, "So that is the Danish King. Who protects him?"

The boy looked up at the soldier and said, "I do! We all do! We all protect him!"

King Christian X rode through the streets every day at 11:00 a.m.

After the King had gone by, we went to Nyhavn to look for my dad. I was not very tall and could not see over the heads of all the people in Nyhavn. My mother and father saw each other at the same time. We went towards him and he went towards us.

When we reached each other, my parents looked so happy together that I felt happier than I had ever felt before. You could tell that my mother and my father really loved each other. We found a bench to sit on and my parents talked for a long while. I came away from the encounter with a fantastic loving feeling.

There was lots of activity during the summer of 1944. There were large general strikes all over Denmark. Danish sabotage action was met with counter-sabotage action. There were many revenge killings. There was also a shortage of all kinds of goods.

When my mother went shopping she took me along. She would give me the necessary ration coupons and money to buy the items. Then she sent me into the store while she waited outside.

The shops were always full of people and very chaotic. There were no big grocery stores. You had to buy food from each specialty shop. There were bread stores, fish stores, fruit stores, vegetable stores, etc.

The crowded stores had no system of determining who was the next customer. The shoppers kept track themselves of who was next. Sometimes arguments broke out. The shopper who was next would say in a loud voice, "It's my turn. It's my turn."

The first time I was in a shop, I watched this activity. When I had determined that you had to say, "It's my turn. It's my turn".

I yelled out, "It's my turn. It's my turn."

A kind lady said, "Look, it's just a little boy. He is so small that he has missed his turn."

Then she lifted me up and put me on the counter where the shop keepers proceeded to fill my order. Now that I knew how it was done, I shouted out right away no matter which store I entered. "It's my turn. It's my turn." as soon as I was in the door. A nice lady always believed me and placed me on the counter so that I was served right away. My mother never had a long wait outside.

Manse

Manse was my friend Sten's older brother. He was very daring. A couple of times I saw him go inside on a basement railing and jump down. Maybe I will do that some day. (I already jump past the five steps on our apartment stairs.)

One day I went out to play. None of my friends were in the yard. Then I saw Manse sitting on the iron bar which was made to hang rugs. Some of the childrens mothers were standing where I was. One of them said, "Manse is fey."

I thought that meant he was unfair or did not play fair. Many years later I learned that during the Viking age there were women who could see a person's aura and could thereby tell when a person had only a short time to live. Such a person with a short time to live was called fey. If a Viking chief was fey, his followers refused to sail with him. An example is that when Ragnar Lodbrok prepared to make his last raid in England, his wife Kraka (Aslaugh daughter of Sigurd Dragon Slayer) could see that Ragnar was fey and knew he would never return. However I think the woman making the remark about Manse, merely meant that Manse was reckless.

I walked over to where Manse was sitting. He smiled at me and said, "Carsten, can you climb up and sit with me?"

I said nothing because I did not know whether or not I could. I shimmied up one of the upright iron poles and got into a sitting position on the cross bar. Then I inched myself out till I was sitting beside Manse. Slowly I started to lose my balance backwards.

I gripped the bar tighter and adjusted my weight forwards. Oops! That was too much. I fell forwards off the bar but I landed all right, feet first almost. My arms also hit the ground. My right arm was all right. But I hurt my left elbow. In the hospital a cast was put on my elbow. A bone in my elbow had been broken.

My father took me home. It was cold so I was wearing a coat. My left arm was in a sling so the left sleeve of the coat was empty.

When we reached the door to our apartment building Soren was standing there. His eyes widened and he said, "Carsten what happened to you?"

I said, "I fell from the rug beating bar and broke my arm."

Soren replied, "Will they be able to put it back on?"

During the next air raid I went to the basement with my arm in a sling.

My father said, "Going to the basement during an air raid is not much protection. If a bomb hit an apartment building, it would go crashing through the roof. Then it would crash through all five apartment floors. It would explode when it hit the concrete basement floor."

8. THE DANISH POLICE

My mother still worked for Fru Larsen. On September 19 the season for the summer resort was over. The Larsens had a house in Copenhagen. My mother took me with her and we went in a street car. About half way there the street car stopped. A German army truck full of soldiers had parked across the street car tracks. We walked the rest of the way. Or rather, my mother walked the rest of the way because she carried me when I became too tired to walk.

I called Fru Larsen 'Fru Larsen'. I could not pronounce 'Howmester'. When I tried to say Howmester Larsen, I would say, 'Gonno Larsen'. Howmester Larsen was very pleased with that. He said that I said, "God Nok Larsen (Good Enough Larsen)".

With a big smile Howmester Larsen said, "I am Good Enough Larsen."

On September 19, 1944 my father was scheduled to work the night shift but the air raid alarm sounded at 11:00 a.m. This meant my father had to go to work. He put on his uniform and gun and started to bicycle to work. People were shouting at my father as he was riding along:

"Do not go to the Police Station!"

"The Germans are shooting at the police station!"

"Hide! The Germans are capturing the police!"

"The Germans have taken the police station!"

My Father stopped at a police call box and phoned his headquarters. The man who answered the phone had a German accent. He wanted to know who Ivan was, where he was, and what number he was calling from. Ivan hung up without answering. The Germans had blown the air raid siren in an attempt to gather in all the police to the police station.

My Father went home and changed into civilian clothes. Then he called my mother at the Larsens. He told my mother to get ready to leave because he was coming to get us.

Howmester Larsen came home to his house and told Fru Larsen and my mother that he had seen the Germans capture the sea police (the coast guard). All the stores had closed and the workers went home. The street cars and buses were stopped and there was a general strike. The Germans had captured the police station and were rounding up all the police in Denmark.

Police officers from Ivan Jorgensen's precinct. My father is on the far right in the front row.

The street cars started to move again. We went home to Thyregodsway 18. My parents packed a few belongings. Our neighbours came and offered encouragement. Some of them helped my parents pack. Kristiansen on the third floor, offered to hold our apartment keys for us.

I was put into a bicycle seat and my parents got on their bicycles. They were going to try to bicycle out of Copenhagen. In some places, there were gun fights in the streets. There were check points at the city exits where Germans checked identity papers. The Germans were hunting for police officers and my father's papers stated that he was a police officer.

Luckily, the check point at the city border was unmanned. My parents thought that the guards had left their posts to help hunt down police men in the city. My parents were just running with no idea of where to go. We met men on bikes who also turned out to be police wanting to escape from the Germans. Like us, these bikers had no idea of where to go. We were all just running.

After a while my parents began to think of where to go. They decided to go to my father's uncle, Valdemar Pedersen in Hvalso which was 50 kilometers away. Valdemar and his wife took us in and were very nice. Their son Jens, who was also a police officer, had come home. He was married and had a six month old baby girl.

9. HVALSO

While we were in Hvalso, we heard that some police officers who had found a new place to live had their furniture moved to their new places. The Gestapo followed the moving trucks and arrested the officers.

My mother went back to the Valby apartment to get some clothes and a few other things. Kristiansen, the man who held the keys to our apartment, told my mother that one night a Gestapo truck had come to the apartment building. They entered the building and using a flash light read all the names on the doors.

Kristiansen was very uneasy. He thought that the Gestapo were looking for Ivan Jorgensen. He wanted my mother to remove everything indicating that a police man lived there. He said that if the Gestapo broke into the apartment and found evidence of a police officer, it would mean trouble for the residents in the building.

My mother removed uniform parts, papers, police magazines and addresses. When she was finished Fru Kristiansen pointed at an item she had missed; the day-to-day calendar. It said September 19; the day the policemen had been taken.

My father wanted to go to Odense on the Island of Fyn where his parents lived. He would have to take the ferry from Sjaelland to Fyn and then take a train to Odense. His identity papers said that he was a police officer so he would never make it past the check points at the ferry and the train.

My mother and I went back to Copenhagen. There we visited my parents' friend Hans Olsen. He had three boys older than me. They were Werner, Willy and Kell. I had a good time playing with these boys. They were always good to me.

Hans Olsen made new identity papers for my father. They said that Ivan Reinholdt Jorgensen was a gardener. We had to get the papers to my father without the Germans finding them at a check station. So, my mother put the papers inside my shirt pocket.

At the outskirts of Copenhagen, my mother was searched at the check point, but they did not search me. My father was now a gardener.

When my father had travelled to Odense, he sent word to my mother that he needed his revolver. My mother got back on her bicycle and drove back to the apartment in Copenhagen. This time I stayed in Hvalso with my father's uncle. At the apartment my mother went into the basement and retrieved the gun and ammunition from a locker. She wrapped this in a newspaper. Every day on the radio it was announced that it was illegal to have a firearm and that it was illegal to know someone who had a firearm. The punishment in both cases was death.

My mother carried the revolver up to the third floor where Fru Kristiansen helped my mother to sew the gun and ammunition inside a cushion. They wrapped the cushion in brown paper and my mother carried the parcel to the post office. There were about one hundred soldiers just outside the post office. My mother made her way through this crowd, afraid they would stop her and search the parcel. She made it into the post office and mailed the package to my father's parents in Odense. My mother was very relieved when she received a letter from my father saying he had received the parcel in good condition.

10. ODENSE

My mother and I started our trip to Odense. We had been in Hvalso for a month. I found the ferry interesting. As we were approaching Fyn, anxious to go ashore, people moved to the place where we were to disembark. When they were at the place, they began jostling and shoving each other, trying to be first in line. They argued and they yelled. I turned to my mother and asked, "Mother, is this a war ship?"

The woman standing next to us yelled, "This little boy just asked his mother if this ferry is a war ship! You should all be ashamed of yourselves! Stop shoving and yelling and behave yourselves! Calm down and be patient. You will be on shore soon enough!"

On Fyn we caught a train to Odense. We walked from the train station to my grandparents, Farfar (father's father) and Farmor (father's mother) They were Laurits and Johanne Jorgensen. They lived on the fifth floor of an apartment building. We were very happy to be united with my father again. My father's six brothers came and went very often at my grandparent's apartment. An extra son would not be noticed.

The resistance in Denmark had been intensifying. About 2,000 Danish police officers had been captured and transported to concentration camps in Germany. The rest of the police joined the resistance. They continued to receive their police salaries.

Because there were no police in Denmark, the crime rate went up. Murders, theft and robberies increased. In late 1944 the Hipo corps was formed to replace the police. Most of the Hipo came from the Schalburg corps. Some also came from Fri Korps Denmark. The Hipo were organized along the same lines as the Gestapo. But the Gestapo were Germans in an occupied country while the Hipo were Danes operating against their own civilians. The Hipo wore black uniforms and drove black cars. They arrested, tortured and executed resistance people. Sometimes they arrested, tortured and executed normal citizens.

Resistance in Odense was very intense. Also intense, was the retaliation by Nazi sympathizers such as the Peter group and the Schalburg Corpse. Gun fights broke out in the streets between Germans and the resistance, between the resistance and Nazi sympathizers, between the resistance and the Schalburg Corpse, between the Peter Group and the resistance, and between Hipo and the resistance. The Hipo removed the doors from their cars so they could get out of their vehicles faster.

Danish resistance fighters

Danish woman resistance fighter

Sometimes an explosion would be heard from somewhere. One time the Germans found out where a member of the resistance lived and they decided to blow up his house. When they arrived, he was not home but his wife and infant were there. The Germans took the wife out of the house. They would not let her go back in for the baby.

They detonated the explosive charges and the house blew up. The wife dashed into the ruins and found the baby crib. A door had fallen on top of the crib. The crib had supported the door which had become piled high with rubble from the house. The infant was safe and sound protected by the door.

One day a neighbour came in for a visit. He had just come from a coffee shop on the main floor of the apartment building. He said that he had overheard two young women talking in the coffe shop. One womanl had said," I know how I can make $100.00"

The other woman said, "How can you do that?"

The first woman replied, "There is a police officer living on the fifth floor. If I inform the Germans they will pay me $100.00."

After hearing that, my father left. He no longer lived with us. He had gone "underground".

In Odense there was a place where you could keep gardens. My Farfar kept a garden there. I sometimes walked with him to his garden and I watched him work in his garden. I was fascinated with his wheelbarrow. I decided to get myself a wheelbarrow. I managed to get a really nice one; the best in imaginary wheelbarrows. Wherever I went I took my wheelbarrow.

One day I went shopping with my Farmor. We went into a shop that had four steps at the entrance. I could not get the wheelbarrow up the stairs. Farmor had to take one end of the wheelbarrow to help me up the steps. On the way out she had to take one end of the wheelbarrow to help me out. Later she said that she had never been so embarrased in all her life.

In Odense was a great Tower called Odin's Tower. The tower had two platforms. The first was 70 meters (230 ft.) above the ground. It had a restaurant with room for 160 guests. Just below the restaurant was a kitchen. The second platform was 140 meters (460 ft.) above the ground with a great view of the whole island of Fyn.

Odin's Tower

On December 14, 1944 at 6:15 a.m. The Peter group blew up the Odin's tower. The explosion was heard for miles.

Saboteurs

The tower collapsed completely and was so damaged that it could not be repaired.

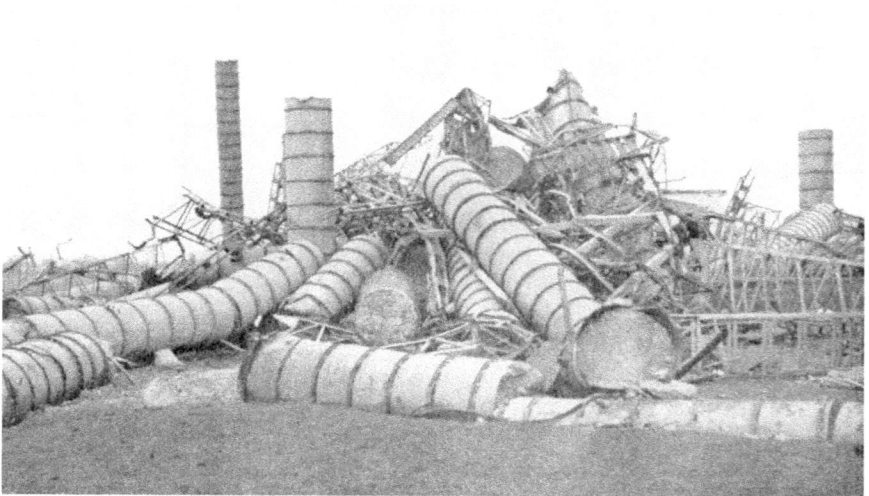

Ruins of Odin's tower

The leader of the resistance in Odense lived right across the street from our apartment. The Germans found out where he lived and a German army truck arrived full of German soldiers. They all entered the house of the resistance leader. He was not home but his wife and infant were home. The soldiers settled in to wait for the resistance leader. We watched from our living room window.

About an hour later, a telephone repair truck arrived. About five repair people went up on the roof of the house. From their equipment bags they pulled out machine guns and started to fire down through the roof. The woman of the house ran outside and threw her baby over the fence to the neighbours. As the soldiers ran outside they were all killed by the machine gun fire. As soon as the soldiers were dead, the resistance fighters dispersed and left the area.

We then saw a man, wearing a long grey coat, limping along the street trailing blood. Every once in a while he leaned against a wall. Then he would continue limping along.

Just then my father entered the apartment. My mother said, "How come nobody is helping that man down in the street?"

My father said, "Nobody wants to help him because he is Gestapo."

I believe that my father had taken part in the action across the street because of the timing of his appearance just when the resistance had dispersed and he knew that the man in the street was a Gestapo.

The wife of the resistance leader found a machine gun in her laundry tub. It had been thrown through the basement window. After an action by the resistance, the guns have to be ditched because the Germans would set up barricades and search everyone for weapons. Anyone found with a weapon would be executed.

The Peter group retaliated the next day. They went into the hospital and executed four doctors.

11. SHELLHUSET

Shellhuset (the Shellhouse) was the office building of the Copenhagen theater. The Gestapo had taken it over as their headquarters. Danish citizens were tortured there during interrogations.

The Danish resistance kept asking the British to bomb it. The British kept putting it off because it was too dangerous. It would require low level flying over a residential area.

Britain finally agreed to bomb the shellhouse. Mosquito bombers and mustang bombers were used. They were supported by fighter planes to take out the German fighter planes and the anti-aircraft guns. The attack took place on March 21, 1945.

British bombers attacking Shellhouse.

The Shellhouse under attack.

The destruction of Shellhouse greatly disrupted Gestapo operations in Denmark. It allowed 18 prisoners to escape. 47 Danish employees of the Gestapo were killed. Eight prisoners also died in the attack. The dossiers and other records of the Gestapo were incinerated.

In the attack on the Shellhouse, Britain lost four mosquito bombers and two mustang fighters and nine airmen died. There was collateral damage. In the first wave of attack, a mosquito bomber's wing hit a telephone pole. The bomber crashed one kilometer away into a boarding school.

A Dane watching a Gestapo headquarters being bombed.

In the second wave of the attack, some of the bombers, seeing the burning school, thought it was the Shellhouse and therefore bombed it. Both the Shellhouse and the school were destroyed. When the school was bombed 86 school children and 18 adults died.

There were other Gestapo headquarters that were also bombed.

12. GOING FOR A WALK

On March 25, my brother Willy was born. Once in a while my mother would put Willy in a baby carriage and we would walk to my Farfar's garden and back. Once while walking back, the air raid sounded. My mother and I walked faster. A man stepped out of a house just in front of us and called for us to come into the basement. He helped my Mother get her baby carriage into the house. I think I forgot my wheelbarrow outside.

One day my father showed up while my Uncle Richard and my Aunt Doris were there. They all decided to go for a walk. My mother took the baby carriage with Willy in it. I walked just behind them with my father, my uncle and my aunt. We had gone about three blocks when the shooting started. Bullets were hitting the walls all around us. We heard the bullets whistle past our heads.

Resistance shooting at Nazis

We did not know who was shooting but there was a fight between the resistance and the Nazis. Uncle Richard and Aunt Doris went and lay underneath a car. My father picked me up and ran. My mother also ran pushing the baby carriage. Bullets kept whistling past us. We made it back to my grandparents' apartment safely and a few hours later my aunt and uncle returned.

13. DENMARK'S LIBERATION

On May 5, 1945, the German troops in northern Germany, Denmark and Norway surrendered to the British and American military forces. The Danish military and Danish resistance fighters, using force, took all the buildings and institutions which had been occupied by the surrendered German forces.

The Danish Brigade and the underground Danish resistance fighters disarmed the German army. My father went back to Copenhagen as a police officer, and helped to disarm the German forces there. They also arrested thousands of German collaborators. There was fierce fighting between the resistance fighters and the Hipo. In Odense 14 Danish resistance fighters were killed. In Copenhagen, 54 Danish civilians were killed and 253 were injured.

On May 8, my mother took my brother in a baby buggy and we went downtown in Odense. The streets were full of people celebrating the surrender of the Germans.

The streets were full of people.

General Montgomery and his Canadian army had entered the city.

General Montgomery in the streets of Odense.

There were thousands of Canadian soldiers. They were driving army trucks and jeeps slowly through the street like a parade. My mother and I tried to shake their hands. We could not really shake their hands though because they kept moving. Instead we high-fived the Canadian soldiers all day. Everybody high-fived the Canadian soldiers and shouted, "Hurrah! Hurrah!"

The people were very happy. I looked into the faces of the soldiers as we high-fived. They looked as happy to be there as we were. They were smiling and laughing and every once in a while one of them would yell, "Hurrah!" I shook as many hands as I could with the high-five.

Montgomery with his Canadian army.

People burned the blankets they had to hang over their windows at night and replaced them with candles.

Danes celebrating the surrender of the Germans.

On the way back to my grandparents we saw people celebrating everywhere.

More people celebrating.

After a while we journeyed back to Thyregodsway 18. My father was back on the police force. Things were a little different than before we fled from Copenhagen because now I had a little brother.

Carsten and Willy

My Father was now in the dog division with the police. Each officer there was assigned a German Shepherd which he trained. Only the dog's master was allowed to train their dog and handle it. My father's German Shepherd was celled Freya (Freya was the Viking goddess of beauty and love). When not on duty my Father brought Freya home with him. I fell in love with Freya.

One day a husband and wife came to visit us. They had a little infant with them. The mother placed the baby on the floor on a blanket. Freya laid down right beside the baby. When the mother went to pick up the baby, Freya would not let her. She growled and bared her teeth at the mother. My mother had to pick up the infant and hand it to its mother.

Willy and Freya

One day, my brother disappeared. My mother was beside herself with worry and anxiety. My father went out to search for him but could not find him. He called the police station and had the police also search for him. Willy was gone the whole day. In the evening a police officer found him. He was in an apartment with two women where he was drinking hot chocolate and eating cookies.

Willy had gone out to play in the yard. But he had not entered the yard. He went on the sidewalk down the street. He crossed several streets and got lost. The two women had found him and determined that this little boy was lost and they took him home to their apartment. My mother was very relieved to get him back.

Now that the war was over I could go back to playing with my friends again. I went to Soren's birthday party in Soren's apartment. My friends Mogens, Ole , Sten, and Jorgen also went to the birthday party. When we arrived, Soren asked, "Did you bring me animals? I have requested animals for my birthday."

On the floor were small toy animals: lions, tigers, elephants, snakes, and crocodiles. We had brought presents and Soren's mother had told our mothers what he wanted, so yes, we had brought him animals.

We sang 'Happy Birthday' for Soren and had hot chocolate and birthday cake. After we had eaten, Soren would not let us touch his animals. My friends, Jorgen, Mogens, Ole and Sten talked together about how disgusted they were with Soren's attitude and then they went home.

Soren was my best friend so I sat down on the floor with him and just watched him play with his animals. After a few hours, I got up and thanked his mother for the nice party and went home.

14. ARRESTS

After the war ended, the Peter Group was arrested. It was discovered that they were the ones who had killed Kai Munk. There are no death penalties in Denmark but after the war exceptions were made. Seven of the Peter group members were sentenced to death in April, 1947. They were executed in May 1947.

About 300 members of the Hipo were prosecuted after the war. About 12 were executed between 1946 and 1950. A large number of Hipo received long term prison sentences.

The only member of the Holger Danske group who survived the war, was Lis Wognsen. She graduated from Christianhavns Gymnasium and went on to study medicine in the University of Copenhagen in 1943. She completed her medical studies in 1952 and started her own practice as an eye specialist in Hillerod. The next year she married a doctor and became Lis Mellemgaard. Her practice lasted from 1952 to 1970. She and her husband had three children.

For many years Lis would not talk about her activities with Holger Danske. In 2008 she wrote her autobiography, "Girl in The Resistance".

15. BALLERUP

My father resigned from the police force. He had saved his money and bought a market garden in Risby Mark per Glostrup. Now he was a real gardener.

Ivan Jorgensen doing some gardening

We moved just outside Copenhagen and rented a house in Ballerup. Our garden was about a 15 minute bicycle ride from our home. We brought Freya with us. German shepherds are one person dogs. The police let my father keep Freya because he was Freya's one person. She always obeyed my father's commands, but she was our pet and we loved her.

Our family spent the next four years living in Denmark which had once again become a peaceful country. When I was nine we moved to Canada and left our beloved country of Denmark to start a whole new set of adventures across the ocean.

Carsten R Jorgensen

ABOUT THE AUTHOR

Carsten Jorgensen was born in Denmark and experienced much of his early childhood during the chaotic times of World War 2.

A few years after the war was over, at the age of nine, he moved with his family to Canada.

Upon graduation from Queen's University in Kingston, Ontario in 1966, he accepted a biologist position on Lake Temagami with the Ontario Department of Lands and Forests.

In 1996 he retired and now enjoys spending his time playing chess, playing darts, doing Tai Chi, and writing books.

If you enjoyed this book by Carsten R. Jorgensen, you may also enjoy these other books that he has written:

The Saga Kings - ISBN-13: 978-0994933805
Trying To Work For The M.N.R. - ISBN-13: **978-0994933812**

Or check out his profile on Good Reads for any new and upcoming books he may be working on.
www.goodreads.com/author/show/14680643.Carsten_R_Jorgensen

www.ingramcontent.com/pod-product-compliance
Lightning Source LLC
Chambersburg PA
CBHW051707090426

42736CB00013B/2578